DEDICATION

This book is dedicated to the families of the author and illustrator, as well as all of those who love Mexico City.

Sacha would like to dedicate this book to Sage and Maddox, who had their babyhood in Mexico City and enjoyed each and every one of these pages in real life, for Colette "Coco" who has only experienced all of the wonderful things Mexico City has to offer from the inside of mama's belly, and of course to David, their daddy, who brought them all here.

Ileana would like to dedicate the book to her husband Carlos "who as a city boy, showed me for the first time the many marvelous things and hidden treasures that beautiful Mexico City has to offer" and to her beautiful son Charlie "who made each adventure in the city unforgettable. I love you always and forever."

Thank you for buying and supporting this book!

ISBN: 978-0692704691
Printed in China
Copyright © 2018 Sacha Xavier Reich

Written By Sacha Xavier Reich
Illustrated by Ileana Pérez-Monroy
Designed by Sabrina Kraus

www.HastaMananaMexicoCity.com

In the markets you'll find all you need at hand.

Hasta Mañana to the piñatas, the tailor, and fruit stand.

The neighborhood markets carry everything from A–Z. It's such a great cultural experience to walk through and shop, especially during the holiday season.

Hasta Mañana to the gondolas as they row.

See you later mariachis singing Cielito Lindo.

Xochimilco (zo–chee–mil–ko) – A neighborhood in México City that has a large canal in which colorful Gondola-type boats called trajineras (tra–he–neh–rahs) sail through with passengers, food, and mariachis – uniquely in México City. Cielito Lindo – One of the most famous mariachi songs, meaning "Beautiful little sky."

Oh Bosque de Chapultepec, a place we love.

Hasta Mañana to the trees and sky above.

Bosque (Boss-keh) means forest. Bosque de Chapultepec (Cha-pool-teh-peck) is the name of the biggest park in México City and one of the biggest parks in the Western Hemisphere. Pre-colonization it was a "retreat" for Aztec leaders. It is considered a historic landmark.

Hasta Mañana, El Bazaar Sábado - where the artists meet.
Watch them paint, buy some art, have a treat.

El Bazaar Sábado, located in Plaza San Jacinto, is a market focused on authentic Mexican art and items. Local artists sell their own work and oftentimes are painting for an audience.

Hasta Mañana to all the vendors in the street.

From lavadoras to tamales to something sweet.

RICOS TAMALES

Lavadoras (lava–doras) – Washing Machines. Kitchen appliances are driven through the street for resale, daily.

Mexico City is full of great museos.

Hasta Mañana Anthropology and Frida Kahlo.

Museos (moo-say-ohs) - Museums. México City boasts 150 museums making it one of the top destinations in the world to see art.

Hasta Mañana beautiful Reforma.

Surrounded by traffic and fountains we adore ya'.

Paseo de la Reforma is a large street that runs diagonally across México City. Some of the city's tallest buildings are on this street.

Hasta Mañana to a place like no other.

La Villa de Guadalupe, devoted to the Holy Mother.

La Villa (La Vee-yah) or Basílica of our Lady of Guadalupe (Gwah-dah-loo-pay) - A historical landmark where an apparition of the Virgin Mary allegedly appeared to San Juan Diego Cuauhtlatoatzin. It is a pilgrimage for many Catholics.

Hasta Mañana Zócalo, the city square.

Until tomorrow, National Palace and flag high in the air.

Zócalo (soh−kul−oh) − The city center of México or "town square." While its formal name is Plaza de la Constitución, most refer to it as Zócalo. The remains of the Templo Mayor (pyramid), The National Palace and a large cathedral are also here.

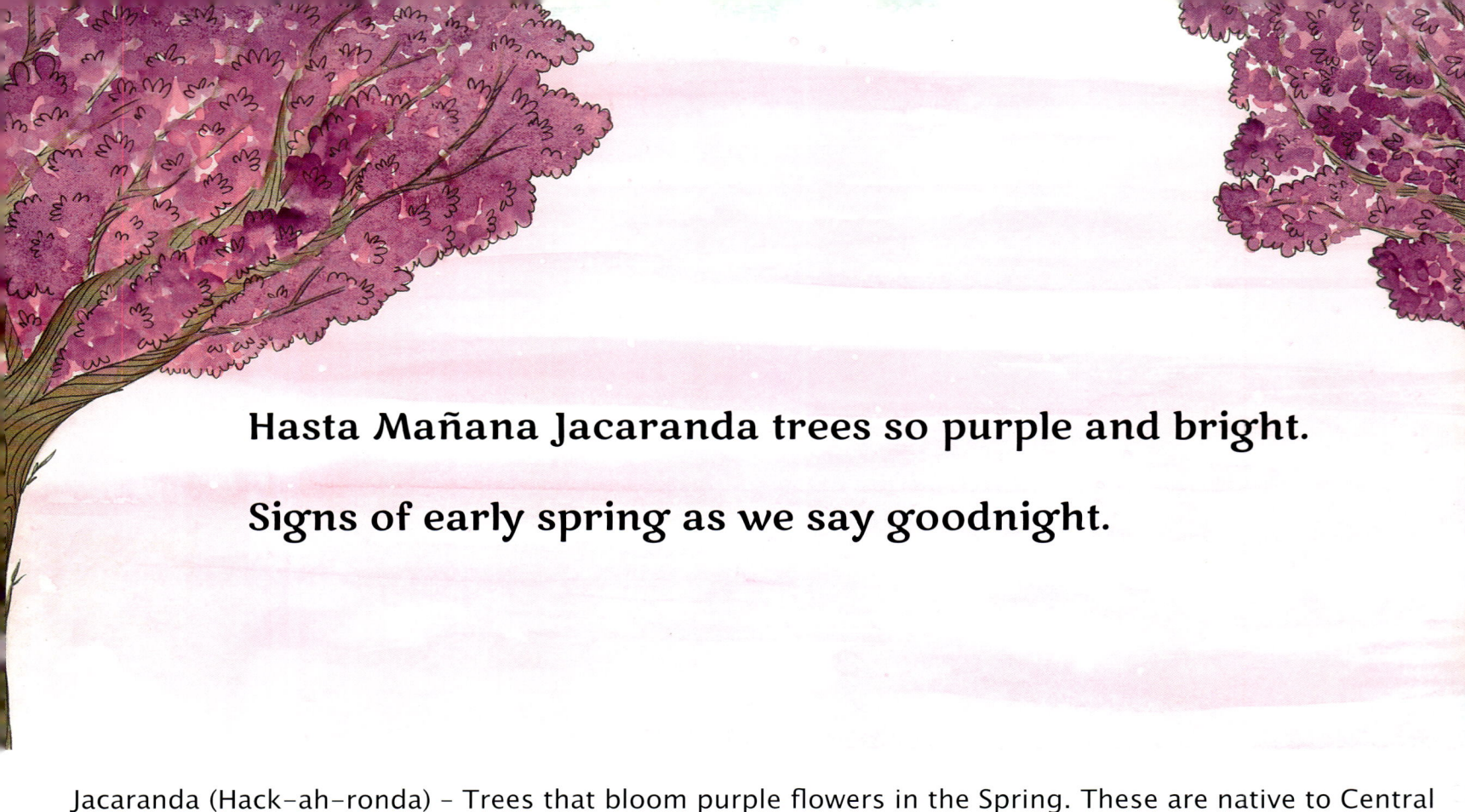

Hasta Mañana Jacaranda trees so purple and bright.

Signs of early spring as we say goodnight.

Jacaranda (Hack-ah-ronda) – Trees that bloom purple flowers in the Spring. These are native to Central America and the Caribbean.

After Halloween we celebrate day of the dead.

With spooky faces, lots of treats, we go to bed.

Day of the Dead – Día de los muertos is a 2-day celebration in which the theme is the after-life but the purpose is to show love and respect for those who have passed away in your family. Mexicans celebrate with colorful face paintings, costumes and celebrations.

Hasta Mañana beautiful streets of Coyoacán.

The sun will rise over the fountain at dawn.

Coyoacán (Coy-oh-ah-cahn) – A park and neighborhood in México City that is the historic center.

Hasta Mañana to the animals in the Alebrijes parade.

They march through the streets and always amaze.

The legend of Alebrijes (Al-eh-bree-hez) – A true legend of a man, Pedro Linares, who dreamt of fantastical figures while very ill. When he woke up he created what he had seen and it drew attention. Every year there is a parade where participants recreate his dreams with papier-mâché animals throughout the city.

When we hear the whistle in the street it means camote.

Time for bed,
Hasta mañana,
Buenas noches.

Camote (Cam-oh-teh) – Sweet Potato/Yams. In México City, on many evenings there are vendors in the street selling yams with a special whistle that blows to let everyone know.

Hasta Mañana pyramids of the sun and moon.

Until tomorrow, lights down, see you soon.

The Pyramids of Teotihuacan (Tay-o-tee-wah-cahn) are an ancient MesoAmerican city which are now the site of astoundingly well-preserved pyramids that once were the villages of the ancient people. It is a short day-trip from the city.

The angel in Reforma watches over the city all night.

Hasta Mañana, sweet dreams, turn off the light.

About The Author

Sacha Xavier Reich and her family moved to the Condesa neighborhood of Mexico City from Manhattan's East Village in New York City in 2013. At the time, her oldest daughter was only 8 months old. As she and her husband David navigated the city for work and pleasure, they marveled at their daughter's perspective of everything she absorbed in this vibrant city. The following year their son was born in Mexico City, creating even more experiences for their family.

The capital of Mexico will always be a special place for Sacha and her family, and this book was written as an homage to the city through the eyes of a child.

She now resides in San Francisco with her family including their third child. They are enjoying all that the Bay Area has to offer but especially the traces of what is left from this original state of Mexico.

About The Illustrator

Ileana Pérez-Monroy is a Mexican artist who quit her English teaching job in a private school in her hometown of Veracruz to become a full time illustrator in Mexico City. It was thanks to the full support of her husband Carlos, who is also an artist, that she felt comfortable enough during the first three months of this new journey to spend as many hours as possible developing her own style.

She now lives in Los Cabos, Mexico with her husband, their son and their two wiener dogs where she continues to illustrate children's books and create art. You can find more of her work on Instagram @pensamientostreet or @ilemonroy

Sacha and Ileana met in Mexico City and created this project together.

www.HastaMananaMexicoCity.com